Blue Rûna

Blue Rûna:
Edred's Shorter Works Vol. III
(1988-1994)

Edred

Published by
Lodestar
P.O. Box 16
Bastrop, Texas 78602

runa@texas.net

The cover art is a drawing of the B-type bracteate of Lellinge (Denmark) dated around 500 CE. The runic inscription reads either **salu-salu** (i.e. something given or delivered, repeated twice) or **s-alu / s-alu** (i.e. the Sun + **alu**, repeated twice).

Contents

Introduction

The *Green Rûna* (1993) and the now rare and difficult to obtain *Black Rûna* (1995) were the first in a series of anthologies of my works which have been produced in often obscure journals. Despite the obscurity of their original appearances, these contributions have been judged by many to be of general value and interest. Hence they are anthologized here for a wider readership.

The contributions in this little book have come from the far corners of my efforts in writing short pieces for outside publications. All of the articles have been slightly updated, and in some cases substantially revised, from their original forms, as noted.

"The Way of Woden" was published in the Fall 1988 (#9) issue of the now defunct *Gnosis* magazine. This article stands as it was written.

"How to be a Heathen" was first published in the journal *Idnunna* in the Yule 1992 issue of that magazine. This is the official journal of the Ring of Troth, an organization dedicated to the revival of Germanic religion. *Idunna* continues to be published today. The final section of this article has been substantially expanded.

By far the most talked about single piece in this anthology is the now infamous "The Secret of the Gothick God of Darkness." It has even been reprinted on various "Goth" websites over the years. It was originally published in the 31 October 1994 issue #6(66) of the now defunct magazine *Fringeware Review*. Besides a few minor corrections this article stands as it was originally written.

"The Alchemy of Yggdrasill" was originally printed in an obscure journal: *The Crucible*, edited by R. L. Barrett. Only two issues of this journal were ever produced. This article has been substantially revised and edited from its original form to reflect more current understandings.

As a final note, access to the text of the much anticipated *Red Rûna* is only by written request addressed to the author care of the publisher of this book.

Stephen E. Flowers
January 13, 2001
Woodharrow

How to Be a Heathen:
A Methodology for the Awakening of Traditional Systems

The following paper was generated from a talk delivered to the Pagan Student Alliance of the University of Texas at Austin, November 22, 1991 and is dedicated to the memory of Edwin Wade, Óðinsgoði, who died on this date in 1989.

I have come to you to speak about *how* exactly one might go about being a heathen, or pagan, in today's world. What I will say will be of use on two fronts. First, it will provide a model for the rationally intuitive "reconstruction" or revival of heathen religions — or better said — cultural value systems. But second, it can also act as a sort of manual of "consumer guidance" for such systems. Since we are swamped with the "marketing" of such systems on a constant basis, I think the time has surely come for some discussion on how we should approach them.

The whole issue of *culture* is often glossed over, especially by American writers. This is because there is usually only tenuous understanding of what all is meant by this term. When we speak of culture, we may meaningfully break it down into four types of culture— all of which blended together give us a true picture of any given historical society, ancient or modern. There is: 1) *ethnic culture,* 2) *ethical culture,* 3) *material culture,* and 4) *linguistic culture.* These may be conveniently illustrated as in Figure 1.

Ethnic	Ethical
Material	Linguistic

Figure 1: The Culture Grid

All kinds of culture have to do with *contact* of some kind between real people. Humans are cultural animals. To survive we need to absorb, intellectually and consciously, tremendous amounts of cultural data. The faculty to generate culture and to absorb its contents is one of the things that separate us from the "other" animals. (Which is another way of saying what makes us something other than animals.)

Ethnic culture is a purely physical reality. It has to do with the reproduction of the carnal human reality — physical bodies — through sexual contact. It is, if you prefer the term, the "racial culture" of a people. In any holistic understanding of culture this must, of course, be accounted for and discussed. When we look around the world today, we see cultures like Japan which has an almost entirely homogeneous ethnic culture. This is also reflected in other aspects of their over all cultural model, which is to be expected. They constitute a true *nation*, in the original meaning of that word, i.e. a people sharing a common birth (from Latin *natio*, I am born). The United States of America on the other end of the spectrum, is not a true *nation* but rather a multi-national *state*.

Ethical culture is the most complex kind of culture. It touches all the other types, and is usually what most people think of when they think of culture at all. It has to do with everything that is contained in, and generated from, the minds of humans (in that given culture). It contains the categories of everything from religions to political ideologies, to literary traditions, to economic systems. Ethical culture is the collective ideology — or spiritual systems — of a society.

2

Material culture comprises, on the other hand, all the physical objects created by *art* (i.e. craft). These are the artificial projections onto the physical world of the contents of the mind— of ethical culture. Often we know of a given historical culture *only* by means of the artifacts (objects of material culture) left behind in the archeological record. This is, for example, the case with the "Old Europeans," the pre-Indo-European folk of the far western part of the Eurasian land mass.

Finally, linguistic culture is the language spoken and understood by a people. This is most intimately connected with ethical culture, for especially in the case of cultures of the past it is virtually only through linguistic records that we can determine what the content of their minds — their ethical culture — was. Factors from the material culture also become extremely important here because it is usually only through tangible (i.e. material) records of the lingustic data that we can know the thoughts of the people of the past as directly as possible— through *actual* scrolls, papyri, inscriptions, books, etc. This is how they can speak to us most directly and most clearly over time, and we must hear them in this way to be sure of the voice of the past.

What most heathens, or pagans, seem to be interested in is the revival of ancient cultures. They like to go back in their minds and imaginations to a time when the cultural grid was a holistic one— where one could speak of (just to name one example) the Germanic culture as a whole: Germanic folk, Germanic religion, Germanic art, Germanic language were one organic whole. If a sense of this wholeness can be regained, it can again make a positive impact on the individual and the culture to which that individual belongs by healing the sense of alienation the loss of that wholeness causes.

This is a noble endeavor. But it is a difficult one to do well and reliably and with a minimum of subjective wish fulfillment. The establishment of a method of doing all this is what I hope to contribute to with this paper.

The "neo-pagan movement" is rife with subjectivism. People reconstruct the "past" in the vision of their own private needs and prejudices. Neo-paganism is often less a religious path and more a system for the validation or justification of subjective biases. Sometimes these subjectives result in effective and sometimes beautiful systems of thought and practice: take for example the original form of Gardnerian Witchcraft. But their bases are nevertheless in the subjective needs and prejudices of the creators. What I propose is the development of an objective, rational basis for a system *from which* reliable and more profoundly useful systems can be developed.

A little less than two thousand years ago, when someone mentioned "pagan science" or "pagan thought" (as distinguished from "Christian") it implied that there was a *rational* basis to it— not a "revealed," irrational one. How much that has changed over the ensuing years! I would like to see the pagan birthright of rationality restored to us. So that when the word "pagan" is heard it will not necessarily call up images of whacked out misfits, but will on the contrary be synonymous with clear-headed, yet inspired, thought.

One of the great pagan thinkers was a Greek named Plato. His system was almost entirely from his indigenous philosophical tradition (although for the sake of prestige he often invented myths about more exotic sources for his thought). Greek idealism, like Indian idealism, is really derived from the same Indo-European ideology. Idealism is, in this context, the supposition that there is a more real, more permanent, world beyond this one, and of which this world is a shadow or reflection. To the traditionalist this is the world of the gods and the world of laws beyond them to which they are also subject. For Plato and the Indian philosophers of the *Brahmanas* and *Upanishads* the world beyond is filled with impersonal first principles, or forms (Greek *eidos*), or archetypes, if you will.

If this world is a reflection or shadow of the ideal world, and if we can learn the laws and principles of how such reflections or shadows are made, we have the possibility of discovering the truth about the hidden world beyond our senses. The way to discover these truths is, furthermore, shown to be a process of *rationally intuiting* the objects of knowledge beyond the grasp of our senses. We begin with what we may know rationally, significantly improve on that knowledge, and *then* jump intuitively (using objective knowledge as our spring-board) into the world beyond the rational. The main problem with pagan

4

thought as usually practiced today is that there is a good deal of jumping— but the spring-board is made of balsa wood.

Plato identified four levels, or types, of knowledge, as shown in figure 2.

Type of Knowledge	Object of Knowledge
4. Rational Intuition	Forms
3. Logic	Mathematical Objects
2. Belief	Things
1. Conjecture/ Guess-Work	Shadows

Figure 2: Platonic Scale of Knowledge

Conjecture, or guess-work (Greek *eikasia*) hardly qualifies as "knowledge" at all. No one should "think" like this. Although all of us do at least occasionally— and most people do most of the time. This is the kind of thought that is based on nothing but totally subjective "evidence," or worse yet, on the subjective evidence provided by others. Two-dimensional characters, such as Archie Bunker, provide perfect examples of such people. Such people know nothing but the shadows or real things.

Belief (Greek *pistis*) is a faith in the validity of things which have been received from authoritative sources. In a traditional society these authoritative sources are easy to identify. The priests and priestesses of the national divinities, tribal elders, etc. In our postmodern world these authorities are more difficult to identify reliably. If nothing else, this paper should be of some use in that process. At this stage the person knows real things, but can only follow certain directions with regard to practice when dealing with things beyond the world of the senses. To this realm belong what we usually think of as "religion"— the correct performance of rituals, etc. This is the level at which the vast majority of people are comfortable. As far as a healthy society is concerned, this is also the level at which most people should be satisfied. Beyond it is a realm of spiritual toil and anguish.

There is a gulf which separates belief from logic. The tension across this gulf was quite palpable in the modern age.

Logic, or rational thought (Greek *dianoia*) is knowledge of the kind we would today call "scientific." It is essentially based on data, which are, as often as not, rooted in mathematics. As we have come to learn in the modern world, if you "have the numbers" concerning something it is likely that you will be able to manipulate or reshape that thing. You can control it because you have quantified it. To this realm of knowledge we would today ascribe all of the arts and sciences taught and researched at our universities. Universities are temples to *Dianoia*— or thought. Today credible knowledge seems to end here. Beyond it lies only mumbo-jumbo and ufo-ria. But such was not the case in pagan times.

Rational intuition (Greek *noesis*) is the highest kind of knowledge. But one can not leap from belief into rational intuition— one must pass through *dianoia*. Long training in objective science (in whatever field) is necessary to cause the mind to function in a reliable manner. Then when it is prefocused on more "spiritual" objects the knowledge it gains will be maximally reliable— or real. We no longer have traditional schools for training in this kind of knowledge. All the schools which exist at present in cultures derived from European roots are new schools. So the question becomes one of quality, not age or legitimacy of authority.

This scale of knowledge, and this whole discussion of pagan bases of knowledge in general, has been offered to give some sort of context for the body of this presentation. The point will be that the "reconstruction" of whole cultural systems must (at least according to the best kind of pagan knowledge) be based on objective criteria and data, but additionally they must just as much be matters of actual *doing*— not merely ivory tower theorizing. It is only through enactment of theory that knowledge becomes real. We can only learn the most important things through action and experience.

How is it that we know how to put men on the moon, or how to build bombs that can destroy the world (proving that we are indeed gods of the planet) today — but we — as a species — in fact know nothing more about the most profound human problems of Love, Truth, Justice, etc. Than did good old Plato? "Progress" can be seen clearly in technological fields because this kind of knowledge (technical knowledge) can be passed on easily in a system of belief from one person to another, from one generation to another. Each person, each generation, does not have to "reinvent the wheel." But when it comes to those other things, those things which cannot be passed on by authority from one person to the next, every person does indeed have to reinvent his or her own wheel. But not just any wheel will do. It has to be the right wheel. This is what *initiation* is all about. This further points to the methods used by philosophers which really can only put the student in a place where knowledge can be gained directly from the source. The teacher cannot impart the knowledge, only create the conditions in which knowledge can flow into the student's conscious mind.

Can a Dead Cultural System be Revived?

Before beginning our quest, we must refine our goals. To the basic question of whether a truly dead cultural system— such as the Egyptian, Sumerian, or Indus Valley — can be revived, I think the honest answer must be: "No." That is, human creativity can (re-)create something of an artificial likeness of such a cultural system to vivify it with action and devotion. But the thing itself is not actually brought back to life. This is in part also due to the fact that in the cases mentioned above the lines of continuity of ethnic, ethical and linguistic culture have been irreparably broken.

But to a slightly different question of whether a sleeping cultural system can be awakened, the answer may more confidently be given: "Yes." If there is come continuity between the past and the present in all four cultural areas— but if a cultural system has nevertheless become disestablished— then it is said to be not dead but merely sleeping. Such is the case with the Germanic tradition. We form a continuously identifiable ethnic unit, we hold to many of the old ethical traditions (see everything from concepts of "English common Law" to the "Christmas" tree), we still create art based on Germanic concepts of abstraction, and we certainly still speak a language derived directly from that of our pre-historic

7

ancestors. None of these categories is completely dead— all are just sleeping under a blanket of Christian/Middle Eastern overlay. The same could be said for the Celtic, Italic, Hellenic, Slavic, and a dozen other traditions. In many ways what I will present in the sections that follow is the method I used in the awakening of the Germanic tradition in a score or so books I have written on the subject, and the methods used for awakening slumbering practices and beliefs in the Asatru movement as a whole. This methodology is essential for students of any such cultural system.

The Process of Awakening

The process of awakening comes in three phases. These do not follow in the linear pattern 1-2-3, however. That is, you do not start in Process I, finish it, and then move on to Process II, etc. Really we are involved on all three levels throughout our lives as long as we are dedicated to the long process of reawakening the hidden reality within. But, with all this being said, wisdom must be applied at all times to discipline one's self so that in the early part of one's quest most of one's time is spent on Process I, while relatively less time is spent on the latter two. As the years do on the balance will begin to shift, and relatively less time will be spent on the objective tasks and more time will be spent in the activation of what one has learned. It is in this latter stage that true understanding arises.

Process I is one of rational discovery or objective analysis— where the traditional record is examined in a scientific manner.

Process II is one of subjective synthesis— where the data gathered and analyzed in the first process are allowed to sink into the subjective universe, or soul, or the individual. Here it is allowed to become whole with your mind.

Process III is one of enactment— where the inner synthesis is activated, made to become effective in the objective universe.

8

Process I
Rational Discovery or Objective Analysis

To begin the first process we have to ask ourselves one basic question: What do we have to work with objectively? Now at this stage we must remind ourselves that we are sticking to things that are part of the *objective* record. What so-and-so might have "channelled" concerning the true nature of the old Germanic, or Celtic, or Egyptian system is, whatever else it might be, not objective. To accept such material or ideas is simply to believe in the power of that individual to "channel" such things. You are dealing with "revelations" not traditions.

So what are the kinds of things that can tell us about the objective tradition? These are mainly *written* sources for reasons outlined above. Does that mean that everything that was ever written by or about a culture is to be used without discrimination? Certainly not. Discrimination is of the highest importance. The sources must be used in the following order or precedence:

1. Internal Contemporary Texts
2. External Contemporary Texts
3. Archeological Evidence
4. Internal Surviving "Texts" (e.g. folklore)
5. Secondary Texts
    a. Autochthonous
    b. Comparative

Internal contemporary texts are ones such as the *Eddas* or runic inscriptions which give us some sort of direct insight into the minds of heathen Germanic peoples. External contemporary texts are things such as the Roman and Greek historians' and ethnographers' accounts of the people indigenous to the north. Although their views may be skewed for one reason of another (and these reasons must be examined) they did have more direct sources of raw information perhaps than we can today, and so remain tremendously valuable. (For a collection of these see James Chisholm's *Grove and Gallows* [Rûna-Raven, 2001].)

Archeological evidence is mute. It can not "talk," that is, convey verbal information, without corroboration from textual sources. If a statue of an otherwise unknown god or goddess is dug up somewhere, and it cannot be identified with some figure in the local mythology as recorded in texts, what are we left with? All that remains to us is some pretty wild speculation based on nothing but an *image*. But if that same artifact is to some extent "explained" by a textual source, then it becomes a great window into the spiritual life of the people.

Again, this bears reiterating, all we can objectively know about a bygone culture must be found in an objective record— written or archeological — and all interpretations of that record must be held to judgments based on the objective record. To proceed otherwise is simply to be a believer in modern prejudices and prophets. To illustrate this was a concrete example, of the many rune books that came out in the 1980s (with one exception) only my works were based on the actual tradition of runology well-known from the runestones, rune-poems, and modern scientific runology itself. All the others freely altered or dispensed with (or more accurately, were simply ignorant of) the traditional knowledge available in any good reference book on the subject— if you couldn't be bothered to visit a runestone. But books were written on the bases of these wild speculations, prejudices, and wishful thoughts. How to decide "which" runic system to use? In a way, I was face with this same problem when I started my own esoteric studies. But I realized that all foundations had to go back to *some* objective piece of evidence — to some runic inscription, to some Eddic or runic poem, to some saga passage, and perhaps to some comparative evidence — all else was interpretation. But as I came to see it, it had to be interpretation *based* on the *whole* of the tradition, not just one select part of it.

Another slightly different class of primary evidence is provided by folklore. By folklore I mean customs, stories and all kinds of traditions that have been handed down in a continuous fashion from early times. Examples of this kind of evidence would be folk-tales collected by the Brothers Grimm or the various country customs collected by folklorists throughout northern Europe. It is probably true that a great deal of this goes back to pre-Christian, heathen, times. The problem is we can never know exactly how much of it has been innovated or imported in the Christian era. Therefore folklore evidence must be considered as being secondary to the more

10

archaic material. It can be used to fill in gaps in our knowledge, but on the evidence of folklore alone no reliable objective system can be created, nor can folklore evidence be used to overthrow the evidence from more archaic sources.

Finally actual secondary, scholarly, literature *about* the traditions must be considered. The huge body of scholarly work that has been done on the ancient Germanic religion, for example, is too rich and thought-provoking to ignore. The present-day heathen should approach this literature as a record of contemporary men and women trying to make some *rational* sense out of the primary evidence according to certain *intellectual* rules by which their science is supposed to be governed. "Inspiration," so important to the practicing heathen, is of much less importance to the scholar. But often inspiration can be drawn from their sometimes limited conclusions. When making use of secondary scholarly literature you should try to find the most recent works possible. If the scientific aspect is being developed as it should be, the older literature will be accounted for in newer, and the older will have been superseded by the more comprehensive findings of the newer as well. The only caveat here is when some ideological fashion (e.g.. "political correctness," "feminism," etc.) comes to dominate scholarship in certain sectors. Learn to recognize and avoid such intellectual fashions. In general secondary material can be divided into two classes: one which treats a given tradition from within itself and another which tries to compare one system to another thereby illuminating further the more obscure of the two. Of course, this latter method must account for the ways in which one system or tradition might be connected to the other. It is in this area that the work of Georges Dumézil is so important.

Now that we have reviewed the types of sources to which we will attempt to gain access, the problem arises as to what exact questions will we attempt to answer with this data. The essentials of understanding any person individually, or any group of people collectively, lie in knowledge of their view of the world, of themselves, of any gods or goddesses they might have, and in understanding the practices they use to act and interact within these various contexts, e.g. what rituals, spiritual technologies to they use.

11

In technical terms we must discover the traditional cosmology used by the folk-group in question. That is, what is their view of the *order of the world*. Also essential to this is the origin of the world, their cosmogony. Once you understand how people view the world, you have gone a long way toward understanding the very soul of the people.

The soul must also come under direct examination. Here we must try to reconstruct the traditional *psychology* of the group. The investigator should try to determine what the folk-group thinks a human being is in essence and how the individual relates to the whole (society and world). This in turn opens the door to the sociology of the traditional group under investigation.

Usually a special category is enjoyed by the gods and goddesses of a people. The divinities are special exemplary models for human behavior and spirituality. By knowing the pattern inherent in the god-forms as well as understanding how the various god-forms relate to each other inside the system we will have a deep-level map of the ideas of the people in question.

Also essential to the whole process is an understanding of the "spiritual technologies" used by a people to communicate with their gods, to interact with them and/or with the world directly. Peoples usually have rituals and customs to effect this part of life. Such customs and behaviors are usually at the center of revivalist efforts. The problem is often that the rituals are lost or only survive in sketchy outlines. At this stage we are primarily concerned with finding out what these outlines are. The only way to restore the soul to these outlines, and to flesh them out again in a robust fashion, is to discover the soul of the people through the understanding of the cosmology, psychology, sociology and theology— and then *enacting* the ritual elements regularly and physically. When modern heathens make the same sounds, gestures or motions that their ancestors did in worshipping the gods or carrying out some other spiritual or magical practice, their actions physically and actually *resonate* with those of the past. The more this is done, the stronger the resonance becomes. This is why in the True movement, or in Ásatrú, it is so often emphasized that actually troth is a matter of *doing*, not believing. From action comes faith in the results of action.

Two other important ways to recover the soul of the ancestors, and ways theoretically very much akin to the rediscovery of their spiritual practices, is the learning of the archaic languages they spoke, e.g. Old Norse (Icelandic), Old English, and/or learning their methods of crafting things in the physical universe, e.g. metal-working, weaving, wood-working. At first these seem to be merely technical undertakings, but as time goes on the soul of the activity will manifest itself as the acts of today begin to *resonate* with the actions of the past and a sort of inter-epochal harmony begins to arise in the soul of the modern heathen.

Process II
Subjective Synthesis

Once suitable progress has been made in all phases of the first process, all the data collected in that learning process is to be constantly and thoroughly submitted to a threefold model of subjective or internal inquiry. Each piece of data is to be considered as it relates to the individual self of the subject (you), how it relates to the tradition (as you have come to understand it), and how it relates to the environment (social and natural). The question of tradition handles the problem through time (diachronically), while the question of the environment handles it as it relates to the here-and-now (synchronically). This process is actually a description of how the individual soul makes sense of the tradition.

As an example of this, let us take the traditional fact that the cosmos is made up of "nine worlds." How does this relate to my individual self? How does this relate to tradition? How does this relate to the world around me? Now let it be said that *what* exact answers you come up with are perhaps less important in the beginning than the fact that you have posed the questions to yourself and set the wheels of inquiry into motion. In time the questions will be answered — not because you read them in a book by Edred Thorsson or Georges Dumézil — but because you have come to *know* the answers yourself. You will have *experienced* the answers.

Often the best efforts at objective and subjective inquiry come to an impasse. Knotty problems sometimes remain. At times, but especially when such thorny problems arise, a threefold tool of inquiry can be brought to bear. Ask these three questions:

1) Is it factual? (i.e. fits the findings in Porcess I)
2) Is it aesthetic? (i.e. pleasing to the sensibilities)
3) Is it useful? (i.e. fills a basic contemporary need)

Again, let's take a concrete example to illustrate how this is supposed to work. Let's say Uncle Einar, who resentful of his Christian upbringing, objects to having a "Yule-Tree" in the hall during Yuletide because he thinks it is a "Christian thing." You want to do the right thing, so you apply the threefold question to it: Is it factual that the tree is pagan? Yes, that can be proven from many sources. Many Christian denominations realize this and therefore try to discourage their followers from having "Christmas trees." "But just because heathens did it doesn't mean we *have* to do it, right?" persists Uncle Einar. This is true, O avuncular one. But the fact that the whole culture finds the tree an important and meaningful part of the Yuletide festivities (despite the attempts of the early Christians to suppress it) shows that it is generally pleasing to the sensibilities of most folks. Because of its popularity its usefulness as a symbol and as a religious practice is assured. It helps us focus on the immortality of the folk so long as its identifiable organic existence continues. Gifts given to the children, and to the ancestors, focus our attention both on the roots and to the leaves of the tree. This also points the way to the preferability of using *living* Yule-Trees. The roots were cut off when the crypto-heathens had to remove their Yule-Trees indoors to worship in secret ways that had formerly expressed in public and in the woods. Let us restore the roots to the Yule-Tree!

So the problem of the Yule-Tree seems to be a personal one for Uncle Einar. He is, of course, free to dispense with it in his own home, but it can certainly be proven to meet all three criteria for continuance, maintenance and redevelopment as a true custom.

Process III
Enactment

Once a set of practices beliefs and so on, have been established through the application of Process II, it increasingly becomes the responsibility of the individual to prove the results of the second process through *enactment*, through actually and physically acting out the practices. This first comes on a personal level. Only through enactment in the physical world can the final judgment be made on the viability of the system you have arrived at. Things that looked good on paper, or sounded good in your head, may be unworkable in actual practice. This can only be shown through practice. On one level this is the end of the whole process, but on another level it is just the beginning.

This process of enactment itself comes in two main phases. The first involves individual enactment. Begin to enact the subjectively synthesized patterns on an individual basis— both internally and externally. Internal "action" is just as important as external action. Internal action is tantamount to faith or belief— a firm conviction of the truth of something. A thought profoundly held and conceived is a powerful deed. Most forceful and sustainable external action is motivated by the emotional engine of the soul, which is perceived as faith or belief. The Norse term for this is *trú*. This moves the subject to act. The external actions may range from undertaking traditional handicrafts with spiritual intent, to the enactment of the religious rites rooted in ancient Germanic patterns, to the carving of runes. Again the important thing is to *act*, and to act in full awareness of the meaning of one's actions. The resonance built up between one's actions and the original paradigms upon which these actions are based is rooted on the trueness, or accuracy, of their forms.

Using these methods you can create your own personal religion, of course. But heathendom is in essence a folk religion, it involves a community of people. Individual development is important and essential, but if it is isolated and detached from others, it will not have permanence, and hence will not be as holy as it might have been. Therefore, the next arena of enactment is on the group level. Unless you can make what you have arrived at up until now valid for a group of people, all you have done is create a highly personalized system. It is for this reason that organizations are necessary in the applications of these methods. Once the system becomes successful for a whole group of people it can be said to have gained, or regained, a transpersonal validity. This is the end-goal of all reawakened heathen systems. When group-level validity is achieved and maintained it becomes clear that the system is not the clever invention of a single individual, but rather the resonant and true reawakening of something that had been slumbering in the souls of all it touches. It can be said to ring true.

The Alchemy of Yggdrasill

I. Alchemy of the North

The Northern Tradition understands well the principles of alchemy. Its very cosmology, cosmogony and eschatology are expressed in formulas any alchemist could understand— if they have learned to ask the right questions. This methodical investigating of the mysteries (*reyn til rúna*) of how things are created, developed and transformed is keyed, like so much else of the Hidden Heritage, to the ninefold paradigm. This ninefold symbol, with *significant* variations, is also known in traditional Northern studies as the Valknútr– Knot of the Chosen, or Slain, or among the Persian brethren as the Naqsh— whence the Gurdjieffian "Enneagram."

Alchemy is a technology of transformation not limited to any one kingdom of existence— it can transform mineral, vegetable, animal or spiritual "substances." There is no one formula for this technology— even the classical western alchemists of the Middle Ages and Renaissance used variations in their formulas. We will learn nothing of practical value if we simply impose the classic alchemical formulas upon data foreign to them. Independent data — such as the traditional cosmogonic process of the ancient North — can teach us new formulas if we proceed in a precise way informed by inspiration.

In a practical sense what appears here is a formula for the *generation* (creation) of any desired thing— be it an object, situation or state of being.

17

II. Northern Cosmogony

The ancient Germanic cosmogony is most clearly and continuously outlined in sections of 2-19 of the *Edda*, written by an Icelander named Snorri Sturluson around 1222 CE. Although ostensibly a Christian, he was far more interested in preserving the heritage of his Northern ancestors than he was in any form of Church (or even Classical) teaching.

The *Edda* tells us that in the beginning there was nothing but *Ginnunga-gap* (magically charged void). This interpretation of *Ginnunga-gap* was offered by the great Germanic philologist, Jan de Vries in an article published in 1930 in the *Acta Philologica Scandinavica* (vol 5). At the southern extreme of this void arose Fire (Muspellsheimr) and at the northern extreme arose Water (Niflheimr). These polar opposites were attracted to each other. As the Fire neared the Water, Space (Air) manifested— through which sparks flew toward Niflheimr. But as the Water of Niflheimr neared the center it hardened (and expanded) into Ice, which contains solid Salts and extrudes from its essence a Venom— which is struck by sparks of Iron. These sparks activated a Yeast (living substance) in the liquefied Ice. [Note that the Ice contains three substances: Salt (solid), Venom (vapor) and Yeast (liquid).]

Where these elements converge in the mild midst of Ginnungagap, there arise two beings from the dripping Ice: first Ymir (a proto-humanoid form) and then Aðumbla (the cosmic bovine). Ymir lives on the milk produced from Aðumbla's udders and she lives by licking the Salty Ice. Out of the Ice Aðumbla forms the shape of a second humanoid: Buri. Buri replicated himself asexually and thus Borr came into being.

In the meantime Ymir also produced other humanoid entities: under his left arm here grew a pair of humanoids, but his left foot engendered with his right foot a whole race of frost-giants (Old Norse *hrímþursar*).

A daughter of the "frost-giant" Bölþorn, named Bestla, mated with Borr. Borr and Bestla had three sons: Óðinn-Vili-Vé. This is really a threefold but singular entity, who is/are the first of the race of Æsir.

Óðinn-Vili-Vé rebelled and killed their maternal ancestor, Ymir, and from the parts of his form they shaped the cosmic order— arranging the earth in the middle and rationally ordering the rest of the cosmos. The stars, sun and moon are appointed their places, etc.)

The Æsir actually created dwarves to compete the work of physical creation. (This point is clear only in the *Elder* or *Poetic Edda*.)

Óðinn then undertakes the Ordeal of Yggdrasill— he hangs himself on the World Tree in order to gain Runic Knowledge. On the Tree he apprehends the ultimate Mystery, and returns to enact what he has learned.

Óðinn then undertakes the building of an enclosure of the gods (Æsir)— called Ásgarðr.

From Ásgarðr, Óðinn ventures out (again in his threefold aspect) and discovers the natural bodies of human beings. In the text these are symbolically represented as "trees" named "Askr" (Ash) and "Embla" (Elm?). Upon these the threefold Gift is bestowed: Consciousness, Life-Breath and Æsthetic Form.

This brief, and in some places simplified, recounting of the cosmogonic process outlined in Snorri's *Edda* and elsewhere in Germanic mythological texts will serve as a basis for further discussion. A complete study of all the details of the process (which has been undertaken) expands, but does not fundamentally alter the "alchemical" and Ennegonic Formula.

It is clear that the threefold entity known as Óðinn ("Master of Inspired Consciousness") is the first consciously creative entity in this process. He is the result of a synthesis of the polar extremes of Fire/Air and Water/Ice, and so contains all the potential present in the original magical charge of Ginnunga-gap. Óðinn then proceeds to act as the "first alchemist." He takes the base substance (Ymir) and subjects it to an *analysis* (*solve*) — it is broken up and broken down into its component parts and rearranged according to the subjective (semi-conscious) contents of Óðinn's mind and will.

A study of the meaning of the three names of Óðinn-Vili-Vé reveals the Secret here: Óðinn = "Master of Inspired Consciousness", Vili = "Volition" and Vé = "Sacrality" (i.e. the conscious division between sacred and profane– the quality of conscious discrimination). Óðinn is the first individual being with these three qualities: Transcendental Consciousness possessed of Will and able to Discriminate between "this" and "that."

III. Alchemical Principles

In the Germanic cosmogony presented above certain features consistent with those we also know as alchemical clearly emerge. There is a movement from primal unity (a coagulated state) through an analytical process (dissolution) into a trans*formed*, re-coagulated state, each time under the guidance of an increasingly more awakened consciousness. This is carried out through confrontations between polarized qualities most simply explained as concepts of Form (Water-Ice, etc.) and Energy (Fire-Air, etc.).

The Germanic cosmogonic mythos provides a doorway to learning of the Secret of *how to bring things into being*. This doorway can be unlocked by those who learn how to use the ninefold key which opens it.

᾽ The primal, or first, unity is Ginnungagap. In it all things are contained. It is beyond all limitations of time and space, in it are unified in a completely undifferentiated way all polar opposites— Ginnung is the absolute unity of Form Mass and Energy. The cosmos emerges from this undifferentiated chaos and returns to it on a cyclical basis.

Before any conscious, or even living beings can come into existence, four pairs of opposing elements must be manifested and activated:

Form		Energy
1. Water	-	Fire
2. Ice	-	Air
3. Iron	-	Yeast
4. Salt	-	Venom

The first two pairs (1-2) manifest the concrete order of the cosmos, while the second two pairs (3-4) constitute the manifestation of living information in the natural cosmic order. Most of the cosmic ordering is made up of substances and processes restricted to the first two pairs. The living information (genetic code) dynamically, but still from our perspective unconsciously, evolves to a point where enough information (from Ginnung) has been cross referenced to make a mutation into a semi-conscious being possible. This is the first of the Æsir: Óðinn-Vili-Vé— the first reunification of the spectrum of all the qualities present in Ginning.

However, this (re-)unified entity is not yet a fully conscious (divine) being. His first impulse is to rebel— to destroy the root from which he sprang and to reorder it in a way more in accordance with his will. This is the first self-aware act of creation. The creation is carried out under the guidance of a conscious and rational plan. Here all the hidden and mysterious laws of nature are laid down. Essential to the process is that the "old order" was deconstructed (Ymir killed and dismembered) and a new order established (from the parts of the old order) according to the subjective will of the creator.

Having established certain laws of nature — that is, archetypal processes — which take on lives of their own, the Æsir create a host of agents of formation (dwarves, or dark-elves) which act as the craftsmen who bring into physical reality the ingeniously fashioned principles of the Æsir. The dwarves are well-known in Germanic mythology as the craftsmen of the gods.

They are the technicians who execute the plans of the gods, but who are also freed by their semi-conscious status to create all manner of forms (including mutations and manipulations of mineral substances, as well as vegetable and animal species). In this process the Æsir are absent as they have withdrawn into another dimension to contemplate the next, most momentous alchemical work.

Óðinn emerges from his withdrawal to undergo the Ordeal of Yggdrasill— in which he extends the essence of himself throughout the structure of the world-order which he has fashioned — he contemplates his own Self through the World-Tree which acts as a multi-dimensional mirror of that Self. The culmination of this act is the apprehension of the ultimate Mystery (Rûna) and the gaining of real Runic Knowledge.

This moment of realization that there is something greater than that of which the Æsir were conscious when they first shaped the World is the result of their contemplation of the entirety of the Work. The possibility of something even greater than self-awareness arises— and although the keys to this

Mystery are imparted to Óðinn (in the form of the Runes) it is also clear that these are *only* keys and that an eternal Quest is necessary to actualize them.

All Knowledge gained in this Quest is then used as a program for further development as well as for the creation of further plans for the evolution of the original creation.

The first act Óðinn undertakes with this new Knowledge is the building of Ásgarðr— a separate, shielded fortress in which the experiment in divine evolution can be carried out.

But this separate fortress, which transcends the mundane universe, must be grounded. It must have a form or vehicle in the mundane universe for purposes of its own evolution, and it must also have a direct connection with the mundane, or horizontal, universe itself.

In order to effect this link, the threefold Odinic entity ventures out from Ásgarðr and takes the natural bodies of human beings (really nothing more than ape-like creatures) and endows them with the threefold Gift of Consciousness, Life-Breath and Æsthetic Form. Perhaps the reason why they are symbolized as trees is that these humanoid creatures were, at that point purely creatures of *appetite*— serving a function little more significant than eating and excreting.

But endowed with the divine Gifts, humans (*mannoz*) become *Agents of Consciousness* in the horizontal plane. What the dwarves were to the creation of the natural cosmos — helpers and allies — human beings are to the continuing creation of the non-natural realms.

IV. Anglular Alchemy

Angles are complex entities. They are essentially defined by two lines which converge at a given *point* in space and which can be further defined by the precise quality of the relationship one line has to the other (e.g. the number of degrees between the two lines). There are also many *hidden* dimensions behind each angle.

Those who have studied the Seal of Rúna will have suspected the nature of the ninefold key to unlocking this alchemical process: An aperture between the original unity of Ginnungagap and the realms of manifestation is created by the first angle (chaos). This chaotic unity is broken by the second angle

22

(order) which describes the manifestation of the four principle elements (Water/Fire/Ice/Air). The third angle (knowledge) manifests the patterns of life and establishes the pathways of information.

A second unity is established in the fourth angle (being) as the life/coded information process engendered in the third angle is completed in the form of first beings capable of self-knowledge. The ring of nature and the trapezoid are completed with the forging of the fifth angle (creation) as the Æsir rebel against the established order, overthrow it and create the cosmos anew in their own images. The sixth angle (death/sleep) is a moment of stasis for the Æsiric creators as they allow their demiurges, or craftsmen, the dwarves, to finish the physical cosmos according to the principles established by the Æsir in the creation of the dwarves themselves.

In the seventh angle (birth/awakening) the Ordeal of Yggdrasill is completed wherein Óðinn becomes conscious of something greater than himSelf, and something which laid outside his consciousness when he reshaped the World (in the fifth angle)— this something is the Mystery (Rúna). This initiatory experience transforms Óðinn into a god among gods. He is conscious as is no other god of his own *limitation* and even *ignorance*, he learns to see more and more clearly and to dream yet more inspired visions of what the divine realm could be. This leads him to design and have constructed the Enclosure of/for the Gods, Ásgarðr, as an idealized community of conscious entities. This is a place where he plans for them to evolve and develop, and is indicative of the eighth angle (re-creation). The re-creation is not a carbon copy of the first creation, it is now informed by a Sense of Mystery (Rúna) and other information gained in the experience of the seventh angle. Ásgarðr is, however, the ultimate staging ground for Becoming throughout the Worlds.

The process first set into motion from a perviously unknown, or unarticulated, original point *begins* to come full circle when the threefold Gift is bestowed upon a natural creature— *Mannaz*. However, this process, the *subject* — the enactor — of which is the Flame, cannot come full circle until the Gifted Race brings it full circle of their own volition — through initiation. This ultimate realization of the source of consciousness, the Flame, closes the cycle and in so doing shall create a new race of gods.

V. Conclusions

One of the essential Runic messages of the exploration of this process is the alchemical Necessity of returning to the roots of things in order to transform them. The exhortation *Reyn til Rûna* mandates a return to the essential, original Forms of things, constantly synthesizing them with the subject's present state of Being. This often necessitates the periodic, and perhaps only temporary, rejection of tradition for its own sake. This process creates a moment of pure Wakefulness, and having awoken, the initiate sees, and having seen the initiate acts effectively with knowledge.

In this article we have presented the outlines of a guide to the successful completion of a complex creative process— any complex creative process— whether it is building a house or creating a new universe.

The alchemical theory presented here is not only a key to the creation and transformation of things/phenomena in the "objective universe," but also a structural map to certain aspects of the subjective universe— the self which is the true *subject* of initiation.

This study is far from a complete discussion of the alchemical Mysteries present in the Ennegonic Formula of Yggdrasill. What you have before you is not an end, but only an eternal beginning, with so much more to discover than what we already know about the process, what lies in Skuld looks to be full of power and wonder.

The Way of Woden
The Runic Mysteries of the Hidden God of the North

Woden, known among the Norse as Óðinn, is the mightiest of the Germanic gods. He is master of magic, skald-craft (poetry), and ecstatic techniques. He is also seen as the ghostly and terrifying leader of the wild hunt and the ecstatic band of warriors known as *berserks*. Woden is the primal ancestor of the royal houses of the north— the Anglo-Saxon kings of England counted themselves as descendents of Woden. Even in ancient times this high god of the Germanic peoples — the Germans, English, Dutch, Scandinavians and the now vanished Goths — was a figure that inspired fear and terror as often as he did awe and deep reverence. For Woden embodies all the mysteries of the human psychophysical complex with all its wonderful contradictions and paradoxes, as well as its virtually unlimited power and capabilities. In understanding the mysteries of Woden we can begin not only to comprehend the timeless and archetypal character of the hidden god of the northern world dwelling eternally within his people, but also to grasp the universal mystery of the human psyche. Like no other traditional god, Woden is the god of the eternal quest of the human spirit to become, and to gain knowledge and power over itself and over nature.

The first key to the mysteries of Woden is found in his name. "Woden" is the English form of the name ultimately derived from a Proto-Germanic(1) form *Wôð-an-az*, which means the "master of inspired psychic activity." According to regular

25

linguistic rules of historical development, *Wôdanaz* becomes Woden in English, Wodan or Wotan in German, and Óðinn in Icelandic, where the initial "w" drops off before certain vowels (hence the form "Odin"). In the Proto-Germanic stem, *wôð*- is the element meaning "inspired psychic activity." The true character of this activity is complex. It can mean anything on a continuum from the furor of battle frenzy to the reflective inspiration resulting in a finely crafted skaldic poem. (By the way, skaldic poetry is perhaps the most complex form of poetry known in any language.) The spiritual quality implied by this characteristic reveals why Woden is not only considered the high god of the Germanic peoples, but is also known as the "All-Father" (ON Alföðr)— for he, along with other aspects of himself, imparted this gift to humanity.(2)

One of the chief sources for Woden's won inspiration and knowledge — for which he has an insatiable thirst — is the perhaps "shamanistic" initiatory ordeal he underwent hanging on the World-Tree, Yggdrasill (= the steed of Ygg/Woden). In this process, discussed in some more detail below, Woden grasps and integrates runic knowledge. The actual meaning of the word "rune" (Proto-Germanic *rûnô*) is "mystery" or "secret"— only secondarily does "rune" represent the visible signs (i.e. elements in a numinous code) which magically help in the understanding and utilization of the true mysteries of which the signs are an outer manifestation.(3) It is the hidden code embodied in the runes which serves to guide Woden's own initiatory path, and it is that when he imparts to his kith and kin here in Miðgarðr or Middle-Earth.

Woden: the Living God

In ancient times it was Woden among the gods who most often intervened in human affairs— sometimes with shockingly tragic consequences. He continued to do so even after the coming of Christianity— although he usually acted from behind one of his many masks. In the last two hundred years he has progressively emerged from behind his various masks until we can say that in our own era no other god from antiquity has shown himself to as vital and purely alive as Woden. The most dramatic — and ultimately the most tragic— outbreak of this vitality was in the German-speaking areas of central Europe during the first half of the 20th century. To be sure not all that happened in that time and place was the inspired work of Woden! The stream of Woden's vitality was broad and deep and was, unfortunately, misdirected by those who did not really understand it.

This stream of vitality first rushed forth through the German Romantics culminating in the *Gesamtkunstwerke* of Richard Wagner. It became more focused in the neo-Germanic movements founded by such men as Guido von List, Otto Sigfrid Reuter, Jakob Wilhelm Hauer, and others.(4) In the 1930s this was so strong and apparently so strongly connected to the Wodenic archetype that C. G. Jung was moved to write his essay "Wotan" in 1936. In it Jung writes what is not only a profound analogy for how the archeype of Wotan was re-emerging but how any inherited archetypal pattern can also:

> Archetypes are like riverbeds which dry up when the water deserts them, but which it can find again at any time. An archetype is like an old water-course along which the water of life has flowed for centuries, digging a deep channel for itself. The longer it has flowed in this channel the more likely it is that sooner or later the water will return to its bed.(5)

The Nazi episode was ultimately an enormous set-back for the remanifestation of Woden. But the stream had not begun to flow with the Nazis and it did not end with them. By the late 1960s and early 1970s movements dedicated to the revival of the ancient Germanic religion in Iceland, Germany, England, and North America were in full swing.(6) In North America this movement is now being carried out by a number of organizations, including the Ásatrú Folk Assembly, the Ásatrú Alliance and the Ring of Troth. Along with this, but largely independent of it, has come a runic revival, led in great measure by the efforts of the Rune-Gild. Slowly and imperfectly some were beginning to feel their way back to the true roots of the mysteries of Woden.

It is clear that Woden is alive— perhaps more so than any other ancient god. Furthermore, his unique character and the fact that he is/was the high god of the dominant ethnos in the world today make it very important for us to seek to fathom his mysteries. The will to power and to self-knowledge embodied in Woden must be recognized, understood and directed— for it will not be denied — if the future is to hold out any promise for us.(7)

The Archetype of Woden

Many pat attempts to pigeonhole Woden in the manner in which other traditional divinities can be treated have been unsatisfactory either because they ignored certain aspects or because they did not seek deeply enough to the essential core of wholeness. This problem is understandable once the traditional sources are consulted in all their complexity.

In the mythology the visions of Woden give us an initially perplexing image. He is seen in Valhalla — as a beautiful youth and as a wise gray-beard upon his high-seat overseeing the great feast of the gods high atop his tower-gate — *Hliðskjálfr* — gazing out over all the worlds. He is also seen as the ferry-man of the souls of the dead. While in visions of those in Midgard he is most often glimpsed as the leader of the wild and ghostly hunt, or as a simple landloper wearing a blue-black cloak, a broad-brimmed hat, and carrying a staff or spear. This latter image is probably very ancient, as he shares many qualities with his closest Greco-Roman counterpart, Hermes-Mercury.

Woden often appears as one of a member of a triad of gods when he is engaging in initiatory or creative activities. These triads all go back to a primeval three-aspected form of Woden, which would have appeared as *Wôðanaz-Wiljôn-Wîhaz* in Proto-Germanic, but which appears as Óðinn-Vili-Vé in Old Norse. Other triads are: Óðinn-Hœnir-Lóðurr, Óðinn-Hœnir-Loki and Hár ("the high-one")-Jafnhár("the equally-high-one") and Þriði ("the third-one"). All of these represent threefold hypostases — aspects or extensions — of the god Woden.

The mythology shows Woden to be the highest god of the Germanic pantheon, the All-Father of the gods and humanity, the lord of battle, the god of the dead and the transference of the dead from this world to other realms, the lord of initiation

28

and transformation, the god of shape-shifting, the patron of skalds (poets), the father of magic, the primeval rune-master, a great seer and visionary— and ultimately an unpredictable deity when viewed from the limited perspective of humanity. It can be seen why for many the god defied classification. However, once focus if shifted to the human psyche as the realm in which the god is truly at home, great possibilities for understanding open up.(8) For us the god's primary name indicates, and all of his characteristic actions show, that he is the god encompassing the internal and external struggles and quests of the human soul.

The many names of Woden open further doors of understanding. In one poem in the *Poetic Edda* called the "Grímnismál" (the Sayings of the masked-One), the god reveals a whole catalog of over fifty names of himself. Over 120 such names have been counted throughout the tradition. The meanings of these names range from the "Worker of Evil" (Bölverkr) to the "All-Father" (Alföðr), from the "God of Cargoes" (Farmatyr) to the "Father of Victory" (Sigföðr), from the "Wakeful" (Vakr) to the "Sleep-Maker" (Sváfnir). His names show multiple dimensions in extreme bipolarity. Among the most revealing names are the ones such as "Changeable One" (Svipdal), the "Truth-Finder" (Sanngetal), and the "Hidden God" (Hroptatýr). The bewildering diversity of Woden's names coupled with the predominance of names having to do with things of the soul and hidden things, demonstrate in the warp and woof of their meanings that this is a god in whom extremes and dualities are brought together — synthesized — in the secret confines of the human soul.

Richard Auld, using essentially Jungian tools of analysis, identifies this synthesizing characteristic as "the integrating bond linking the two opposing halves of the psyche"(9) — e.g. the conscious and unconscious, but not limited to that. The Austrian scholar, Otto Höfler, had already identified two "basic forces" at work in the cult of Woden which he compared to the Nietzschean analysis of the Dionysian and Apollonian forces.(10) Today we might add the model of the right and left hemispheres of the brain to this understanding. The key to unlocking the mysteries of Woden is the realization that even at the very core the Wodenic archetype is not simple— but manifold. In its absolute simplest form it is a bipolar power—emanating from a mysterious and unfathomable wholeness—and returning to that wholeness again and again. It is eternally dynamic and eternally multifaceted. From this core of tripartite wholeness, the initially bewildering multiplicity of forms and functions of the god Woden come into focus. It is a wholeness of being that does not deny the many for the sake of the "one," nor does it forsake its integral wholeness for the sake of multiplicity. Woden is then the god exemplifying the ability of the human psyche to synthesize and integrate the parts into a whole— the objective as well as subjective realms.

Another key to the mystery of Woden is to be found in the various symbolic animal figures ascribed to him and which surround him in mythic iconography. He rides the eight-legged steed Sleipnir (Slipper), he is accompanied by his two wolves Geri (Glutton) and Freki (Greedy), he is attended and advised by this two ravens Huginn (Mind) and Muninn (Memory). He is also connected to eagle forms: one of his names is Arnhöfði (Eagle-Head); and to the serpent: two of his names Ófnir and Svávnir, may mean "snake." This array of zoomorphic symbols also points to the all-encompassing character of Woden, who is in the midst of these symbols— the eagle, is that of sovereign power, the ravens of the bipolar (cognitive/reflective) intellectual faculties, the horse of the power to traverse the worlds (or dimensions), the wolves of the appetites for pleasure, and the snake of malevolent destruction (or defence). All of these possibilities of expression are constantly arrayed around the essentially threefold character of Woden— which is at once integrative, transformational, and separative.(11)

In examining the complex activities of Woden in his mythology, Einar Haugen identifies three major areas of concern: death (by which the mysteries of magic and transformation can be understood), war, and şsex for fun."(12) But we can go beyond this to see that Woden's concerns are essentially fourfold: 1) wisdom and magic (which include the central mysteries of the death), 2) war and defence (in his warlike and royal aspects), 3) "management" (of the orderings of gods, humans, and nature), and 4) sex (both as All-Father progenitor of gods, demigods and human society, and as a purely fun activity. This latter aspect is so prevalent in the mythology and didactic poetry ascribed to Woden that is must be said to hold a preeminent place in the Wodenic mind-set. (Even a god can't spend all this time brooding over the fate of the cosmos high atop his tower-gate!)

The Ancient Cult of Woden

The way of Woden is something more than mythic patterns recorded in ancient poetry and sagas. Most of the myths are reflections of cultic practices or examples of the wisdom — practical and speculative — preserved within this cult. The way of Woden first and most powerfully emerges in the historical records concerning the Erulians and Goths. The Erulians were not a tribe in the usual sense, but rather a cultic league of wandering warriors dedicated to Woden who ranged all over Europe from the Black Sea to Britain, and from Scandinavia to Italy during the first centuries of this era. Perhaps the runes did not originate among them, but they were so widely used by this group that the title "Erulian" became a common designation for "runemaster" in the oldest runic inscriptions, where the word appears as *erilaz*.

The tribal god and mythic progenitor of the Goths was Woden. One of his names in Old Norse, Gautr (Gauts in Gothic) means essentially "father"— and it is reflected in the name of the tribe. The Goths, although some of them were ostensibly (Arian) Christian by the fourth century, carried their Germanic mystery traditions throughout southern Europe from the third to the sixth centuries. They, and related tribes such as the Vandals and Burgundians, founded Germanic kingdoms in Italy, southern France, Spain and North Africa. Among the Goths, as among the early Anglo-Saxons, there was a strong tradition of sacral kingship. This stemmed from the belief that the kings (really the aristocracy in general) were direct, genetic, descendants of the royal god, Gauts— Woden.

It is, however, only from the so-called Viking Age (800-1100 CE) that we are able to obtain detailed evidence for the internal nature of the mysteries of Woden. The myths containing these details are for the most part to be found in the *Poetic Edda* (many stanzas of which go back to the 8th and 9th centuries) and the *Prose Edda* of Snorri Struluson (1222 CE). From the

31

older evidence it seems clear that the way of Woden was a continuous tradition carried from at least the very dawn of this era to the coming of Christianity to the north— which was not even nominally complete until the eleventh century! After that time the mysteries of Woden went more or less underground to be preserved — if imperfectly — in literature (mainly in Iceland) and in magical traditions throughout the Germanic regions.

The Mysteries of Woden

The Yggdrasill working is reflected in two stanzas of the "Hávamál" (Sayings of the High One) in the *Poetic Edda*:

> I know that hung   on a windy tree
>   all of nights nine,
> wounded by a spear   given to Woden,
>   myself to myself—
> on that tree   which no one knows
>   from what roots it rises.
>
> Neither bread they dealt me   nor drink they gave;
>   netherward I looked—
> I took up the runes,   took them up roaring,
>   I fell then back again.
>   (Hávamál 138-139)

This is a reflection of an ancient ritual initiation in which the candidate is suspended in a tree (possibly in inverted position), tortured and starved— coming to the brink of death — whereupon the runes (mysteries) are seen, grasped, and learned. Then the candidate returns to the realm of the living with his wits and knowledge intact. In undergoing this, or functionally similar initiatory rites, the candidate in the mysteries of Woden is emulating an exemplary model provided by the god himself.

On a more abstract level the key to these stanzas lies in three factors: 1) the process describes, 2) the sacrifice, and 3) the knowledge. The process involves a departure from the realm of the living, from normal sustenance, and from physically comfortable conditions. There is a separation into a ninefold "space"— the nine worlds of the World-Tree— and for a ninefold period of time. In this cosmic space/time the work of transformation takes place (sacrifice and integration into the mysteries). Then there is a return to the world wherein the effects of the work of transformation are to be manifested. The sacrifice itself is a curious one and is described in what is perhaps the most profound half-line in the *Poetic Edda*— myself to myself (*sjálfr sjáfum mér*). To emulate the god's exemplary actions the candidate does not sacrifice himself, or anything else, to the god— but rather to his own self. This is the mysterious catalyst allowing for the runic initiation— the inward turning of the focus of attention to the self itself wherein the gateway to the runes is to be found. The runes themselves are first and foremost the mysteries— the hidden keys to universal patterns of meaning and power. These are the true objects of the working and the well prepared self is the matrix in which they can initially manifest.

As most commonly understood, the runes constitute a system of writing— just as our alphabet does. But they go beyond this— in a manner very similar to the Hebrew letters. The runestave (or runic letter) is a complex symbolic expression of the rune (mystery). The Table A shows the complete runic system as it was in the earliest phase of its development. There it can be seen that there are many "layers" of symbolism inherent in each runestave: 1) number/order, 2) sound value, and 3) name— with its exoteric and esoteric meanings. The actual "thing" symbolized by this system cannot, of course, be depicted at all— this system is merely the outermost form of it accessible to our sensibilities.

The initiatory assimilation of the runic mysteries is essential to the true character of Woden. It is through this act of grasping the mysteries of the universe and understanding them that Woden actually becomes that which he is— the god of synthesis.

Rewinnng the Poetic Mead

In the myth of the rewinning of the poetic mead, which is recounted in the *Skáldskaparmál* section of the *Prose Edda*,

Woden/Óðinn regains the substance of inspiration. This liquid substance was originally fermented from the blood of a god, Kvasir. This Kvasir was a being created from the combined essences of the two opposing races of gods, the Æsir and Vanir. Thus the "blood of Kvasir," or the "poetic mead" is an essence of inspired synthesis itself. As such it rightly belongs to the gods of consciousness, the Æsir. However, at one point it was acquired by an etin (giant) named Suttung— who has no real use for it but to hoard it. This is much like the serpents who hoard gold for which they have no real use— but they guard it obsessively. Woden's task then becomes to get the poetic mead to Asgard where it will be of use to gods and humans.

The process through which the liquid of inspired consciousness is rewon by Woden forms a pattern of graded initiation itself.

I. Woden/Óðinn, in the guise of Bölverkr (Evil-Worker), gains access to the mountain where the giants have hidden the mead. He does this by breaking an oath not to break into the mountain. Oathbreaking was among the worst of evils possible in ancient Germanic society. Bölverkr teaches the higher law of Necessity which is beyond good and evil.

II. In the form of a serpent Woden bores his way into the interior of the mountain. For this he needs his serpentine form which is capable of traversing the chthonic realm and of penetrating to the heart of darkness.

III. He emerges in the interior space of the mountain where the mead is stored in three vats named Óðrœrir (exciter of inspiration), Són (repayment), and Boðn (container), all of which are guarded by the giantess Gunnlöð. There Woden spends three nights with the etin-wife. As a reward for his "good company" she allows him three sips of the poetic mead. But he drinks the entire contents of all three vats down in three great gulps. Here there is the familiar threefold essence of the mead. The sexual component involving Gunnlöð is also an indicator of the importance of sexuality at this stage of the initiatory process.

34

IV. After Woden has assimilated the poetic mead in its entirety, he transforms himself into an eagle and flies out the top of the mountain to Asgard where he spits the substance out— again into three containers in order to preserve its threefold nature. The mead has now been removed from the realm of the giants to that of the gods— consciousness has been raised from a lower to a higher state of being.

In the paradigm of the myth of the rewinning of the poetic mead we see another essential initiatory pattern within the northern mysteries of Woden. In both the Yggdrasill rune-winning and in the rewinning of the poetic mead, there is the plunge into the depths of darkness— wherein the mystery which is sought for is grasped — whereupon there is a return from the darkness in which enlightenment has been gained.

The way of Woden is a timeless path. Those who follow it rightly do not look to the past as such for their models, but rather to those mythic paradigms preserved from bygone ages which are in and of themselves outside the measure of time. Taking into account what Jung and others have written about Woden, it might be said that he is, and has been for ages past, the true hidden god of the "west." It is indeed Wodèn who has loomed behind the Faustian spirit of the quest for sometimes forbidden sources of knowledge and power. In many regards we are lucky to have so many of the technical aspects of the way of Woden still at our disposal. The myths contained in the Eddas and other sources, combined with traditional forms of runelore and runework, provide the keys to open once again the way of Woden within those who seek the mysteries of the integration of the soul over which he rules.

Primary Sources

Hollander, Lee M., translator and editor. *The Poetic Edda*. Austin, Texas: University of Texas Press, 1962, 2nd ed.

Snorri Sturluson. *Edda*. Translated by Anthony Faulkes. London: Dent, 1987.

Notes

(1) Proto-Germanic is the grandparent language from which all other Germanic languages, e.g. German, English, Dutch, and the Scandinavian dialects are descended. It goes back several hundred years BCE.

(2) This myth is recounted in the "Völuspá" (sts. 17-18) in the *Poetic Edda* and in ch. 9 of the *Gylfaginning* in the *Prose Edda*.

(3) For a complete outline of the runic tradition on an esoteric basis, see Edred Thorsson's works *Futhark, Runelore*, and *Runecaster's Handbook*, all published by Samuel Weiser (York Beach, ME, 1984, 1986 and 1988 respectively).

(4) For a historical discussion of this movement, see Nicholas Goodrick-Clarke, *The Occult Roots of Nazism* (Wellingborogh, UK: Aquarian, 1985) and Stephen Flowers' translation and introduction of Guido von List's *The Secret of the Runes* (Rochester, VT: Destiny, 1988).

(5) C. G. Jung, "Wotan." In: *Collected Works*, vol. 10. Translated by R. F. C. Hull (Princeton: Princeton University Press 1960-1969), p. 189.

(6) See Stephen Flowers "Revival of Germanic Religion in Contemporary Anglo-American Culture." *Mankind Quarterly*, 21:3 (Spring, 1981), pp. 279-294.

(7) For a contemporary perspective on the archetype of Wotan, see Ean Begg, *Myth and Today's Consciousness* (London: Coventure, 1984), pp. 97-106.

(8) Another writer taking this perspective is Richard Auld, "The Psychological and Mythic Unity of the God, Odhinn." *Numen* 23:2 (1976), pp. 145-160.

(9) Auld, p. 147.

(10) Otto Höfler, "Zwei Grundkräfte im Wodankult," pp. 133-144.

(11) Thorsson, *Runelore*, pp. 196-197.

(12) Einar Haugen, "The *Edda* as Ritual: Odin and His Masks," In: *Edda: A Collection of Essays*, ed. R. J. Glendinning, et al. (Manitoba: University of Manitoba Press, 1983), p. 16.

The Secret of the Gothick God of Darkness

There is a Secret God, a Hidden God, who dwells in a spiralling tower fortress and who has guided and overseen our development from time immemorial— and who has remained concealed but very close to us awaiting the "future" time of re-awakening. The time of the reawakening is near. Already we have heard the distant claps of thunder which signal the coming storm.

The legacy of the Dark Gothick God is one which can guide those chosen by him to a state of development wherein they have attained a permanent (immortal) consciousness which is free to act or not act in the material universe as it desires. This consciousness becomes privy to all manner of secrets of life *and* death and life in death. The price for this attainment is contained in the cost of attaining it— for one who has been so chosen there can be no rest, no respite from the Quest which is, and remains, the Eternal Work.

Because the *way* in which knowledge of this Dark Gothick God is passed from generation to generation contradicts the favored methods of the so-called "major religions" of the world— the religions of the "book"— Judaism, Christianity and Islam — this knowledge and its methods have been forbidden and made increasingly tabu for all of the centuries since the cunning ideological conversion of Europe by Christianity.

Books can be burned, religious leaders can be killed— but the blood endures.

37

The Gothick God

In the past ten or fifteen years our European culture (including the "colonies" of western European cultures such as those in North America and Australia) have witnessed a revival of an Æsthetic "Gothick Kulture." This revival, or reawakening, of the Gothick spirit in many respects follows the characteristics of all the previous revivals.

The word "Gothick" is the key to understanding the nature and character of the spirit behind the Æsthetic. (Here I use the "-k" spelling for æsthetic reasons as well as to differentiate the cultural movement from designations of architecture or literary history— more commonly spelled in the standard way.) "Gothick is ultimately derived from the name of an ancient Germanic nation— the Goths.

These Goths came out of the far North (from present-day Götland in Sweden) and swept down into southern Europe beginning about 150 CE. They split into two major groups along the way: the Visigoths and the Ostrogoths. In the south they established kingdoms in present-day Spanish Italy (with its capital in Ravenna) and southern France (with its capital in present-day Toulouse). This latter kingdom, under pressure from the Franks, moved its capital to the present-day Spanish city of Toledo. In all of these regions the Goths established many secret traditions at the highest levels of society. The tip of this secret iceberg is revealed when you see how many names of nobility are derived from Gothic forms. Some of the more familiar examples of these would be Frederico, Adolfo, Carlo, Ricardo. . .

The mystery of what happened to the lost treasure of Rome (including the "Lost Ark") can be solved through knowledge of Visigothic secret history. But that is a story for another time. Eventually the Goths were militarily defeated by a coalition of the roman Catholic Church and the king of the Franks, who was the first Germanic king to convert to Roman Catholicism. All others before him, including many Goths, had "converted" to their own brand of esoteric "Gothic Christianity." The final end to overt Gothic rule in Spain came with the Muslim invasion in 711 CE. But their secret traditions lived on.

The Goths gained reputation in their own time, and through subsequent ages, as a sort of "master-race." In ancient

Scandinavia the word *gotar* was used as an honorific title for heroes, as even today members of the noble class in modern Spain are referred to as *godos* ("Goths"). As time went on, some of the secret Gothic tradition merged with some of the established traditions of the peoples among whom they disappeared, while other parts of it were submerged in the cultural "under-class" of peasants, vagabonds and heretics.

Four to five centuries after their official "demise" an æsthetic in memorial to the spirit of the Goths was created in northern Europe— later art historians even named the style "Gothic." But nowhere the Goths had been remained unmarked by their prestige and secret tradition. This dark and mysterious Gothick past of superhuman qualities loomed as a secret alternative to the bright and rational Classical past which was used as a model for both Christian theologians of the Middle Ages and rational humanists of the Renaissance.

It is in this cultural framework that the Romantic movement began to grow in the 1700s. The Classical models had failed the *avant-garde* of the day. They looked to a more distant past, as a way of looking into a deeper, more mysterious, and at the same time more *real*, level of themselves. When the French looked beyond their Medieval Christian roots they found the Romans, and hence the word "Roman-tic" aptly described what it was they were looking for. In northern Europe, however, the term "Romantic" was generally found wanting by the adventurous souls who saw nothing of the *deep-past = deep-self* formula in the word. It was still remembered that our noble past was not Roman, but *Gothick*. (By now the word "Gothick" was also a synonym for "Germanic" or "Teutonic."

The Gothick world was a world of the distant and powerful past, shrouded in mist and swathed in darkness— a night-side world of dream and nightmare. The Gothick images conjured by the artists of the day— poets such as Burger, Novalis, Byron and Hugo, or painters such as Fuseli, Arbo and Doré— acted as doorways for opening the world to the Gothick steam. The dead came alive once more and walked among the living— and upon the living begat the children of darkness.

This process has continued from those nights to these branching out in ever wider circles to encompass more aspects of life. But at the level of what might be called "popular

39

culture" traces can be seen that connect Ann Radcliffe's *The Mysteries of Udulpho* to M. G. Lewis' *The Monk* to C. R. Maturin's *Melmoth* to E. A. Poe's tales and poetry to R. W. Chambers' *The King in Yellow* to Bram Stoker's *Dracula* and on to Hanns Heinz Ewers, H. P. Lovecraft and Anne Rice. All in their own ways, wittingly or unwittingly, have contributed to the descent of the Gothick God of Darkness in popular culture.

In many respects Stoker's famous novel, *Dracula*, was a "warning" of an "evil influence" from the Gothick past— *Die Toten reiten schnell!* Stoker has his evil nobleman declare his kinship with the northern Berserkers who fought with the "spirit which Thor and Wodin [*sic*] gave them," and even obliquely refers to the Gothic tradition reported by Jordanes in his *Getica* that the Huns were the offspring of Gothic sorceresses, known as *Haljurûnas* (Hel-Runes) and devils that roamed the steppes.

Neither was this influence lost on the American writer H. P. Lovecraft, who, when he was feeling more "heroic" in his younger days, strongly identified with the Gothick heritage. In a letter from October of 1921 he wrote: "I am essentially a Teuton and barbarian; a Xanthochroic Nordic from the forests of Germany or Scandinavia. . . I am a son of Odin and brother to Hengist and Horsa. . ."

The most important god of the ancient Goths was their most distant ancestor, which the Gothic histories record as one named *Gauts*. Old Norse literature provides the key to discovering a more familiar identity of this God. There we find this name among the many given to the God Óðinn or Woden (as he was known among the Anglo-Saxons). Óðinn is called the All-Father, and Gautr is at the head of the genealogy of the Gothic kings just as Woden is at the head of the genealogies of all the pre-Norman English kings.

This God — or ultimate præterhuman ancestor — is a wise and dark communicator. He is the master of all forms of mysterious communication by means of signs and symbols. In ancient times a system of such symbols for communication were discovered, and called "Runes." In order to learn these the God hung himself for nine nights on a tree and thereby encountered the realm of Death— and from that spear-tip point which is the interface between Life and Death he at once comprehended the Runes— the Mysteries of the World.

These Runes form a system of semiotic elements which are not only potent in a purely abstract or theoretical way, but which are, by their very nature, connected to the physical universe and the realm of generation and regeneration.

Even in ancient times, when Woden was acknowledged as the High-God of the Germanic peoples, he was not a very *popular* God. He hid himself from most, and many were glad of it. Then and even now he dwells in deep darkness and travels to the most forbidden zones of the multiverse in his eternal search for increasing knowledge.

As with the ancient Goths, Wodan's most essential role in as the All-Father, as the progenitor of a continuous blood-line— and through that blood-line the forger of a permanent link with humanity. The importance of *blood* as a symbol of what is at the heart of what is going on in a more mysterious way is essential. The mystery and the secret of Wodan is not that "knowledge" of him is passed along through clandestine cults (though this too occurs), or even through the rediscovery of old books and texts (though this happens)— but rather that such knowledge is actually *encoded* in a mysterious way in the DNA, in the very genetic material, of those who are descended from him. This, in and of itself, is an awful secret to bear— and once grasped it is a secret that has driven more than one man mad.

Runic (Mysterious) information is stored "in the blood" where it lies concealed and dormant until the right stimulus is applied from the outside which signals its activation. In this way, knowledge can seem to have been eradicated, but yet resurface again with no apparent, or apparently natural, connection between one manifestation and other subsequent remanifestations.

Scientists have more recently discovered the phenomenal platform for this noumenal process in the form of the double helix of the DNA molecule.

The Secret

The Gothick obsession is an obsession with the Mystery of Darkness. It is no accident, or if it is an "accident" it is a meaningful synchronicity, that the name of the mythic sorceresss of Gothic history that gave birth to the Huns was

Halju-rûnas, which literally translated from the Gothic would be: "The Mysteries of Death." The Gothick offspring have always sought to pry into the Mysteries of Life and Death, to penetrate to the depth of the self and to the outermost reaches of the darkened and chaotic world. Boldly forging into the Darkness to seek the Grail of Undefiled Wisdom, to *Seek the Mysteries*, is the highest Quest of the Gothick Children of the Night. There is great power in the Quest, and in the Quest alone.

The Gothic word for "mystery" is *rûna*. When the Gothic bishop Ulfilas translated the Christian Bible into Gothic for use in the Gothic cult, he translated the Greek word *mystêrion* (μυστηριον) with the Gothic *rûna*.

The practical power of this at once simple and obscure idea of mystery was once well illustrated in an episode of the once popular American television series, *Unsolved Mysteries*. One day an out-of-work father took his sons fishing in a remote forest area where they discovered some stones in the river carved with a variety of arcane symbols. The father and his sons were deeply struck by the signs— What could they mean? Who could have carved them? They went home filled with a sense of mystery awe. Within a short time business opportunities poured the father's way and the family was soon prosperous. They attributed their good fortune to the power of the stones. (Experts from a nearby university determined that the signs were carved recently and were not Amerindian pictographs, thought they appeared to be imitations of similar designs.) Indeed, the family had come by their turn of good fortune from the stones— but not because of the particular shapes or qualities of the signs themselves but rather because of the *sense of mysterious power* which had struck the father and sons upon seeing the stones in the first place.

In the coming years the value and power of the concept of pure Mystery, or the Hidden, will become more apparent as the ways of the Gothick God of Darkness begin to unfold.

That which links this world with that of the Mysterious Gothick realm is clearly symbolized by the blood. But do not mistake the symbol for the entirety of the thing itself— although it, as a true *symbol*, is a *fractum* of the thing itself. The Gothick heritage, the heritage of power and knowledge, is encoded information which is by some as yet unknown paraphysical process passed from generation to generation. Knowledge of this mode of transmitting information is among the greatest tabus in our contemporary society. The reason for this is that it represents the single greatest challenge to the Christian *and* Modern establishments with their dependence on conventional modes for transmitting information (especially the written word). The forbidden secret of the Gothick god is that you can be informed from within, by means of innate structures, which are stimulated by actual experience in the framework of objective intellectual knowledge (undefiled wisdom). When the right constellation of individuals with this knowledge are present the Age of Dependance — on Medieval Churches or Modern Governments — will begin to come to an end. One of the chief signs of the dawn of the emerging new paradigm came on the fifth of May in the year 2000.

The Gothick God of Darkness is the Unknown God, the Hidden God— and hence the God of unknown and hidden things. His actions are hidden because he *is* hidden. Mere words cannot reveal this information, only Words (the hidden forms behind certain key concepts) can do this. It is these which hold the secrets of eternal consciousness and power beyond death. Look, you see it before you now! If you see it, you must work to realize it within— and having mastered it there, to realize it without.

In his landmark work *The Postmodern Condition* the French critic Jean-François Lyotard has some interesting things to say about the character of knowledge and the unknown in the coming years.

> Postmodern science— by concerning itself with such things as undecidables, the limits of precise control, conflicts characterized by incomplete information, 'fracta,' catastrophes and pragmatic paradoxes— is theorizing its own evolution as discontinuous, catastrophic, non rectifiable, and paradoxical. It is changing the meaning of the word knowledge, while expressing how such change can take place. It is producing not the known, but the unknown. (p. 60)

Among the unknown things which will be produced in the Unmanifest zone, which the profane call the "future," will be the engendering of a new Gothick realm which will be none other than the remanifestation of the elder realm. As yet it lives in crimson darkness, but in the spiraling tower the Gothick God waits and watches as those who will call his realm forth work their wills upon the world.

Reyn til Rûna!

Table A

The Runes of the Older Fuþark

No.	Name	Translation of the Name	Esoteric meaning of the Name
1	*fehu*	Livestock, money	Dynamic power
2	*uruz*	Aurochs (wild bison)	Vital formative force
3	*þurisaz*	Thurs (giant)	Breaker of resistance
4	*ansuz*	A god (= Woden)	Sovereign ancestral power
5	*raiðō*	Wagon/chariot	Vehicle on path to cosmic power
6	*kēnaz*	Torch	Controlled energy
7	*gēbō*	Gift (sacrifice)	Exchanged force
8	*wunjō*	Joy/pleasure	harmony of like forces
9	*hagalaz*	Hail(-stone)	Seed form and primal union
10	*nauþiz*	Need (distress)	Need-Fire (resistance/deliverance)
11	*isa*	Ice	Contraction (matter/anti-matter)
12	*jēra*	Year (harvest)	Orbit (life-cycle)
13	*eihwaz*	Yew-tree	Axis (tree of life/death)
14	*perþrō*	Lot-cup	Evolutionary force
15	*elhaz*	Elk	Protective and tutelary numen
16	*sowilō*	Sun	Sun-wheel (crystalized light)
17	*teiwaz*	the god Tyr	Sovereign order
18	*berkanō*	Birch(-goddess)	Birch numen (container/releaser)
19	*ehwaz*	Horse	Twin equine gods (trust)
20	*mannaz*	man(-kind)	Human order of divine origin
21	*laguz*	Water	Life energy and organic growth
22	*ingwaz*	Ing, the Earth-God	Gestation/container
23	*dagaz*	Day	Dawn/twilight (paradox)
24	*oþila*	Ancestral property	Self-contained hereditary property

www.ingramcontent.com/pod-product-compliance
Lightning Source LLC
Chambersburg PA
CBHW031217090426
42736CB00009B/956